A photograph of one of Hartlepool's oldest social clubs, the Engineers, after its 1919 refurbishment – at a total cost of £444 16s!

A rare photograph of Old Hartlepool's temporary lighthouse, erected after the destruction of the original during World War One.

A proud day for West Hartlepool as the statue of one of its founders, Ralph Ward Jackson, is unveiled in front of assembled

ignitaries in 1897.

West Hartlepool townspeople celebrate its being named Jubilee Town and receiving its Charter of Incorporation.

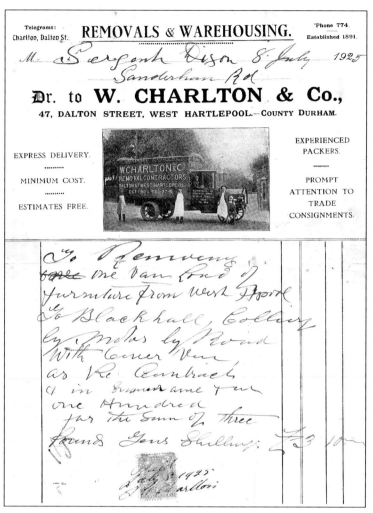

One West Hartlepool family was charged the handsome sum of £3 10s 0d by town removal firm W.Charlton & Co for a job well done in 1925.

What better way to enjoy a 1915 Sunday afternoon than by strolling along Old Hartlepool's promenade.

What better way to end an exciting 1920s day out on Crimdon beach than by washing away the sand with a steaming jug of tea from the resort's thriving cafe. Day trippers enjoy a walk along The Mouth, of Crimdon Dene, summer chalets lining the resort's banks.

This photograph of two of West Hartlepool's best-known characters, street cleaner Teacake Annie and Mr George Hall, was taken around the turn of the century.

These youngsters are dressed up in their Sunday best to celebrate the 1930s opening of West Hartlepool's Grayfields leisure complex.

Magnificent hats abound in this charming photograph of a 1922 Ward Jackson Park garden party.

Days to Forget

A horse and cart struggles past the *Mail's* old Murray Street branch office during serious 1900 West Hartlepool flooding.

Boats share the streets of Stranton with horse and carts as the town copes with more heavy flooding.

Storm damage at West Hartlepool promenade, March 1906.

One of the most famous blazes in West Hartlepool history was the 1949 Seaton Carew propyard fire which left more than 25 acres of the town devastated and required the valiant efforts of 1,000 troops and 25 brigades. Government officials described the 36-hour blaze as 'the biggest concentration of fire appliances since the war' which caused more than £500,000 worth of damage.

More photographs from
the 1949 Seaton Carew
propyard fire.

Another photograph from the 1949 Seaton Carew propyard fire.

Ouch! Not the best of days for these bus drivers.

1954 was the year West Hartlepool lost every match but that has little to do with the town's football club. It was in fact the year one of the town's biggest factories, the West Hartlepool North of England Match Company, went up in flames. The fire was such a spectacle that townspeople bought platform tickets from the nearby station in order to obtain a better view of the night-long blaze. One of the photographs was actually taken from the old *Mail* office, looking across the bus station.

West Hartlepool North of England Match Company well and truly alight in these two pictures.

This dramatic scene was pictured at Billingham railway station in 1953 when amazingly no one was killed. The near-disaster occurred when drivers of trains on the northbound slow line misread the signals.

One of the blackest days in North-East history was Tuesday, 29 May 1951, when 83 men lost their lives in the Easington pit disaster. An underground explosion brought tons of earth crashing down the Duck Bill area of the Five Quarter seam, trapping pitmen (see also next page).

Hundreds of residents left their beds in the early hours and gathered at the pit gates for news of loved ones. It was not until

14 June that the final body was gently brought to the surface.

You can almost feel the bitter cold as these poor bus drivers attempt to dig their way out of terrible 1960s winter weather.

Firemen fight to save trapped workers after a trench collapses at Peterlee in February 1967.

May 1967 found West Hartlepool's Brinkburn Grammar School for Boys devastated by a serious blaze which caused more than £30,000 worth of damage to its main administration centre.

Old Hartlepool's outdoor swimming pool takes a major battering from heavy storms as fascinated onlookers watch.

West Hartlepool has received more than its fair share of heavy flooding over the years as the following pictures show.

More flooding
photographs.

This 1960s AFS exercise at Hartlepool docklands aimed to stimulate conditions arising out of an assumed atomic explosion on Teesside. Water was pumped from various points in the Central and Union Docks which, in the actual event, would be used for the needs of Teesside.

West Hartlepool has seen many dramatic fires over the years – three in particular. Here's the 1978 Lion Social Club fire.

The 1986
P.M.A. Textiles
fire.

The 1970
Reeds
Corrugated
Cases blaze.

Hundreds of sightseers from all over the region headed to Hartlepool in November 1985 to witness the stricken Dutch freighter *The Anne*, left high and dry at Seaton Carew.

What better way to finish this section than some scenic shots of West Hartlepool and Castle Eden in the snow.

The War Years

The Bombardment

On 15 December 1914, a German raiding force – consisting of the battle cruisers *Seydlitz, Moltke, Von Der Tann* and *Derfflinger*, the heavy cruiser *Blucher*, four light cruisers and two flotillas of destroyers – steamed out into the North Sea. The object of the raid was to bombard the fortified coast towns of Hartlepool and Scarborough and to lay mines along the coast. The German plan was for the ships to concentrate their fire for the first 15 minutes on the Hartlepool batteries at the Heugh (two 6ins guns) and the lighthouse (one 6ins gun) with the object of putting them out of action, and then the *Seydlitz* and the *Moltke* were to spend the next 30 minutes leisurely bombarding the harbour works and the town. At 8.10am on the morning of 16 December, the blitz began. Forty-two minutes later, 112 Hartlepool people lay dead and more than 200 were injured after the blackest day in Hartlepool's history.

After the bombardment.

World War One

Unexploded shells fired by the German battle cruisers.

Men of the RGA and Durham RGA who managed the Hartlepool Batteries on 16 December 1914.

Helping the cause in World War One were these ladies from the town's Central Marine Engine Works.

Soldiers from the Devonshire Regiment who were stationed near Hart Village. The above photograph shows some of them outside Hart Smithy while below they are pictured outside the White Hart public house in the village with the landlord John Dixon.

The giant Town Moor bonfire ready for lighting as part of the celebrations to mark the end of World War One.

A rare photograph of Egbert the Tank which was awarded to Hartlepool for the town's war effort fund-raising record.

World War Two

Brenda Road was the scene of wartime devastation.

One lucky Faulder Road family-of-seven escaped without a scratch after their home was destroyed by a 1940 air raid.

The town's greyhound stadium takes a direct hit.

Amazingly, Church Street's Yorkshire Penny Bank survives the German air blitz.

Hartlepool's Box factory was another victim of the August 1940 blitz.

Air-raid wardens survey the ruins of another bombed building.

Families go about their daily business amidst the Studley Road mayhem.

Nine Pilgrim Street residents lost their lives on 30 August 1940 during one of Hartlepools' worst air raids of the war.

A Hartlepool man, John Punton, became the first British civil defence warden to lose his life during this air raid on 19 June 1940 which also killed a woman and badly damaged St Cuthbert's School.

Workmen begin the salvage operation in Musgrave Street after an attack in June 1940.

Together again …Heater and Catcher girls, who worked at Hartlepool's Central Shipyard during World War Two, enjoy their reunion at the Owton Manor Social Club.

Central Shipyard workers take a well earned breather.

Brave North-East men prepare for the 1944 D-Day landings.

Bomb damage at Upper Hart Lane.

A soldier walks past the blitzed Lord Clyde Hotel.

RAF pathfinder John Hodgson was one of Hartlepools' many unsung heroes. This quiet, family man survived 60 operations in his Lancaster bomber. His aircraft is now in Hendon's War Museum.

Bomb-sight Bertha became one of Hartlepools' best known war heroines. Dorothy Robson was just 23-years-old when she was tragically killed in an air crash during World War Two. Also known by RAF aircrews as 'The Girl with the Laughing Eyes', Dorothy carried out important Government work, installing and adjusting bomb-sights in wartime bombers.

One of the most famous sights in post-war Hartlepool was Hitler's Yacht, the SS *Grille*, which was berthed at Hartlepool's Fish Quay until it was dismantled in the early 1950s.

The gallant ladies of Stranton First Aid Post, captured on film as they worked at their duties in 1939 and relaxing in a quieter moment.

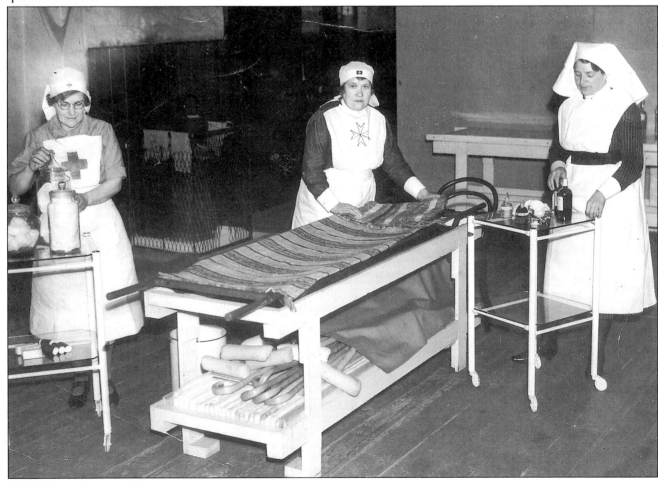

Life on the Shop Floor

Environmental-friendly Hartlepool has always been leading the way in 'green' issues as seen by this 1950s promotion drive.

A huge consignment of beer prepares to leave Hartlepool's Cameron's brewery in 1970.

A light-hearted moment at the same brewery as a coopers' apprentice undergoes an initiation ceremony.

This arduous seven-mile barrel push by Cameron's employees raised more than £1,000 for handicapped children in 1976 and became a popular, if exhausting, annual charity event.

One of the first shifts gets underway at Hartlepool's £52 million South Durham Steelworks. Sadly, much of the plant was to close in the 1980s putting thousands out of work.

Salt comes off the production line at Hartlepool's former Cerebos factory, now known as RHM, during the 1950s.

Police officers line-up to be inspected on a snowy 1960s day.

Hartlepools Laundry and Dye Works Ltd was one of the town's best-known sites until its 1960s closure and eventual demolition.

Movie star pin-ups adorn the walls of Hartlepool's old Match factory which was destroyed in one of the town's biggest fires.

The staff of Hartlepool's Odeon Theatre, 1947-48.

Old Hartlepool's bustling Fish Quay had more than its fair share of characters in the 1950s, as shown above and on opposite page.

Hard at work in the kipper factory.

The 1950s equivalent of a modern-day road snarl-up!

Sea-coaling in the 1970s at Seaton Carew.

Collecting sea-coal at Seaton Carew.

Two former Hartlepool landmarks now long gone. The giant Durham Paper Mill tower bit the dust in the 1970s with the huge Powlett Road gas holder following a decade later.

Sweeping for mines on
Seaton Carew beach.

Galvus breathing apparatus training at Hartlepool Fire Brigade.

Busy workers at Hartlepool's old buttons factory.

One of Hartlepool's best-known annual events – 'tatie-picking' week which tempted many a youngster to bunk off school.

Making sure the post gets through at the old sorting office.

Still going strong –
the traditional
Christmas Santa bus
does the Yuletide
rounds.

One of Hartlepool's best
loved buildings,
Cameron Hospital where
thousands of babies
were born, was sadly
demolished to make way
for housing.

Cameron Hospital exterior and interior.

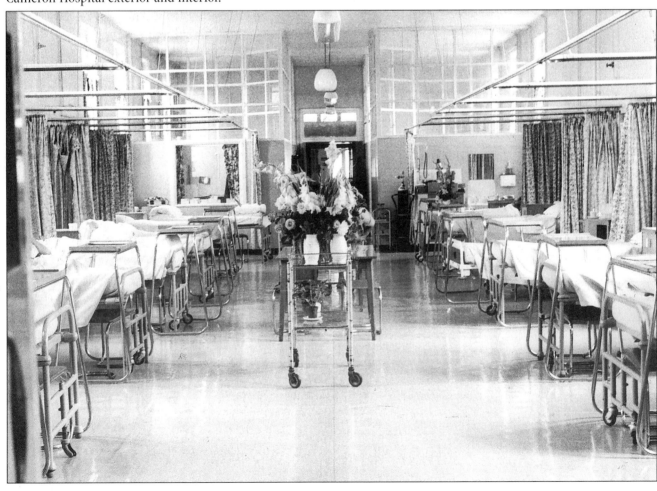

A messy job but someone's got to do it – cleaning the old outdoor swimming pool at Seaton Carew.

Marching for a better future – campaigning seamen fight for improved wages.

The giant Expanded Metal plant in action.

Fashion Industries' workers protest outside Hartlepool's electricity shop over 1970s power cuts.

One of Expanded Metal's more unusual jobs – building road signs for Saudi Arabia.

The bitter 1984 miners strike, which pitched brother against brother, and found wives and children protesting alongside their men.

The 1984 miners strike.

The agricultural side of Hartlepool life is reflected in this fine photograph of a Hart Village farmer tilling his fields.

Foster Wheeler and Head Wrightson are two more shadows of Hartlepool's once glorious industrial past.

Dock Scenes

Sitting on the dock of the bay watching the old coal drilling tower while the long forgotten swan neck crane swings silently.

Hartlepool's once-thriving Coal Staithes.

Graythorp's old ship repair yard. This 1961 photograph shows the intricate ship surgery involved in floating the stem of the *Titanian* away from the rest of the vessel which was then married to part of the *Fabian*.

The dredger *Robert de Brus* at work opposite the lifeboat station.

The much heralded launch of the *Atlantic Countess* in 1954.

The busy office of William Gray shipyards, *c.*1949.

Ships, steel and coal were the mainstay of Hartlepool's once booming docks.

The launching of the Stanpool in the 1950s.

Almost two decades apart, two giant oil platforms slip slowly out to sea after being built at the now mothballed Laings Graythorp yard.

A proud moment for Mayor Councillor Hugh Gardner as he helps launch the Ellerman Lines' container ship *City of Hartlepool* at the Appledore shipyard, near Bideford, North Devon in March 1979.

A birds-eye view of the ship repair yard at Graythorp.

The Royal Mail train steams past the old Hartlepool Rink during the 1960s.

School Days

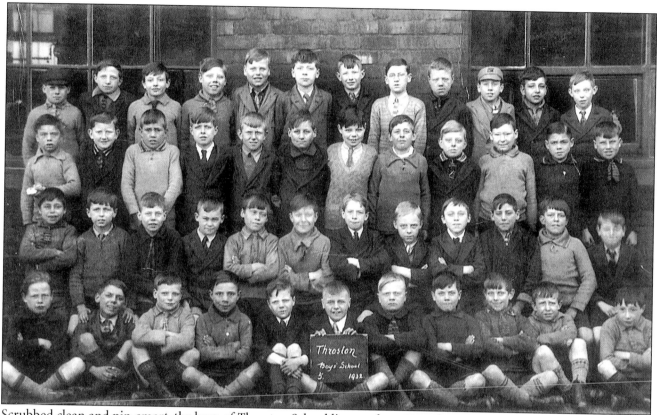

Scrubbed clean and pin-smart, the boys of Throston School line-up for a 1932 class photograph.

Two of Hartlepool's most famous sporting sons, championship winning boxers Jack and Brian London, are featured in this 1944 gymnastics line-up.

A group of Hartlepool school evacuees pictured at Whitby's Mulgrave Castle in 1939. They are photographed with the Marchioness of Normanby, also proudly wearing her gas mask.

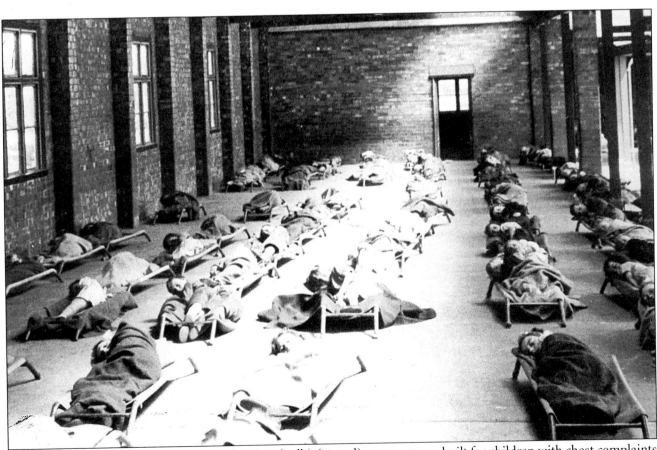

This open-air Thornhill School, with its 'sleeping shed' (pictured), was purpose-built for children with chest complaints and other illnesses. Virtually all glass, the classrooms were designed to let in a maximum of fresh air.

Youngsters at Hartlepool's long-gone Gas Street school enjoy a Victory in Japan tea in August 1945.

Helping the war effort – metalworkers at Dyke House school in 1943.

It's cycling proficiency test day on the town's Old Bull Field.

A proud day for the footballers of St Cuthbert's when they won the double, town champions and cup winners, in 1929.

Pretty as a picture – the girls of Church Close school in 1932.

Forget Frank Sinatra and Elvis Presley – these young Galleyfield School ladies were far more interested in a book on the Lake District during their annual awards day.

One of Hartlepool's oldest school photographs. This wonderful picture of Lister Street school was taken in 1916.

Paying attention and dressed to perfection – Girls' High School pupils during the 1950s.

Hartlepool at Play

Hanging out with friends in the early 1970s.

Was this 1950s bridegroom a pipe welder?

The Mayor rolls a penny at a 1950s garden fête.

Pigeon fancying – as popular today as it was in the 1950s.

North-East political legend Manny Shinwell enjoys a 1950s Miss Crimdon beauty competition.

Youngsters enjoy a street fishing game.

Drill time for 1950s sea cadets.

Enjoying crab boat rides at the Fish Sands during a glorious 1950s summer day.

Smile please – one for the 1950s photograph album.

Enjoying a day out on Seaton Carew beach in the 1950s.

All the fun of the fair at Seaton Carew.

Dressed to thrill at an Old Hartlepool 1950s pageant.

Time for a comic!

Showdown at the Hartlepool Corral but who will the pretty lady choose?

Santa pays a visit to the old Hollymount children's home.

Thousands of miners descend on Durham for its popular gala.

The popular seaside resort of Crimdon through the decades with caravans eventually replacing the old beehive huts and changing tents.

Helpers preparing a float for a local carnival.

Enjoying big band music at the town's Odeon Theatre.

Catching a rare glimpse of Hartlepool's petrified forest.

Supermac (Prime Minister Harold MacMillan0 enjoys a pint with Hartlepool boxing champ Teddy Gardner in the town's Gardener's Arms.

Sulky racing at Elwick in 1969.

Amateur dramatics has always been popular in Hartlepool and this cast shot was taken from the Northgate Methodist Church's 1935 production of *Phyllis, The Farmer's Daughter*.

A day out for members of the Central United Workmen's Club, taken during the late 1960s.

Hartlepool people could certainly turn on the style as this 1950s group shot of the town's Licensed Victuallers annual dinner shows amidst the swank of the Grand Hotel.

This super bird's eye view of Crimdon Lido, taken in 1967, shows the orderly array of holiday caravans flanked on one side by the Coast Road and, on the other, by the tide-resisting cliff.

Greatham youngsters prepare for the village's Bonfire Night celebrations.

Easington MP Manny Shinwell, later to become a Lord, joins proud marchers heading towards Durham Gala.

Children enjoying the pleasant calm of the Burn Valley Gardens' Peter Pan pond.

Future Prime Minister
Tony Blair, then a
fresh-faced Labour MP,
takes part in the 1986
Miners' Gala march.

Winter shopping down
busy Lynn Street,
Hartlepool's main
thoroughfare for many
a decade.

Battling through the mud at Peterlee Show.

One of Hartlepool's best-loved sights – the elephant march as the circus arrives in town.

These happy 1970s children try
their best to carry out a sponsored
silence.

Scooters and trikes are the order of the day as these youngsters enjoy a day out on the Burn Valley swings.

Going for victory at the Rovers Quoit Club.

These members of the town's Ye Olde Durham's Club are looking forward to a charabanc day out in the 1920s.

Graythorp was once a thriving Hartlepool village as shown by these 1930s photographs.

Collins fairground, at Seaton Carew, seen from the air in its heyday.

The Changing Face of Hartlepool

Looking down Church Street from Binns' roof in 1967.

Hartlepool's former equivalent of Harrogate's famous Betty's – Birks Café on the old Station Corner. This popular meeting place was renowned for its tea and toasted teacake.

Once thriving Lynn Street begins to feel the effect of the new Middleton Grange Shopping Centre as long-established companies move base.

Three long-forgotten views of Stockton Street prior to the dual carriageway and Middleton Grange Shopping Centre.

Town drapers Rosens, of Musgrave Street, was the place to shop for many years.

A 1950s shot of the old War Memorial, now impressively restored.

Hartlepool's own 'Coronation Street' view as this photograph looks over the Tower Street rooftops towards Christ Church a

he docks.

It looks a lot different today. The centre of 1950s Hartlepool as viewed from the air.

Grantully Nursing Home, on Westbourne Road, where thousands of Hartlepool babies first entered the world.

Binns crossing, taken in the same decade.

The town's old Skeleton Pier, a former mainstay of Hartlepool Docks.

Old bus shelters outside once thriving Church Street shops.

Another long-forgotten Hartlepool landmark. This time the old Throston Bridge which divided the two Hartlepools.

Old Hartlepool landmark, the Spion Kop refuse destructor chimney.

These rundown Middlegate Cottages, next to Hartlepool Borough Hall, have since been beautifully restored.

St Hilda's Hospital, on the Headland, which was closed in 1984.

The old market
buildings on Lynn
Street.

A sad farewell too as the Middleton Road swing bridge nears the end of its busy life.

Dockers head home down Middleton Road after a hard day's grind.

The old Mothballed Fleet which was one of Hartlepool's nautical landmarks for many years.

A wintry shot of Wood Street, since replaced by the Middleton Grange Shopping Centre.

Houseboats at Greatham Creek.

A rarely seen 1948 photograph of Old Hartlepool's Borough Buildings, now known as the Borough Hall.

The old Water Works which made way for the town's new Brougham School.

Steetley Magnesite, once one of Hartlepool's biggest employers, viewed at its industrial best.

The PDSA's free caravan which treated hundreds of sick pets in the 1950s and 1960s.

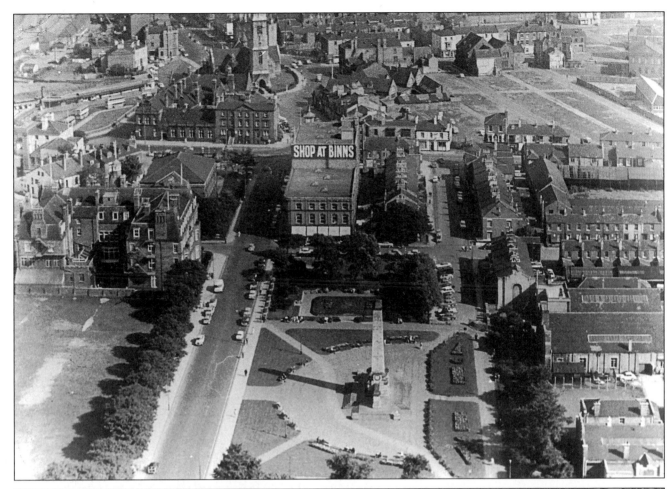

These excellent aerial views of 1960s Church Street in comparison with the same view in 1996 on opposite page.

Hartlepool's multi-million pound marina has had a tremendous impact on Hartlepool, largely due to its successful Historic Quay tourist centre, exclusive Jackson's Landing shopping complex and restored *Trincomalee* warship. These impressive aerial views (previous page and above) show the old bay of Hartlepool before the marina was started ten years ago and the same view from above today.

Our final aerial photograph shows the booming Haverton Hill shipyards during the 1970s.

Political Life

Hundreds turn out to cheer the town's late MP, Ted Leadbitter, as he races to victory in the 1964 election. Tragically, Mr Leadbitter died in 1996 after a car accident.

This historic photograph is the last taken of town council and officials of Old Hartlepool Borough after its amalgamation with West Hartlepool in 1967.

A meeting of the old West Hartlepool Borough Council in the 1960s.

March 1974 saw Hartlepool becoming part of Cleveland County Council and this is a final group photograph of the former Hartlepool County Borough Council. Now, of course, Cleveland County Council is defunct and Hartlepool is once more unitary.

A light-hearted moment in the 1987 General Election found town businessman Leo Gillen naming sweets after each political party.

Sporting Memories

Battling Hartlepool brothers John and George Feeney seen as boys and later showing off their hard-earned Lonsdale belts in the 1980s.

Another pair of champion Hartlepool brothers – Jack and Brian London photographed with their proud father.

A boxing bout being staged outside the town's Engineers Club which was popular in the 1950s.

Top boxer, and future star trainer, George Bowes working out.

One of Hartlepool's greatest-ever sportsmen Dick Ripley who took part in the 1924 Paris Olympics, made famous by the movie *Chariots of Fire*. Mr Ripley, who died in 1996 aged 95, won a bronze medal in the 440 yards relay.

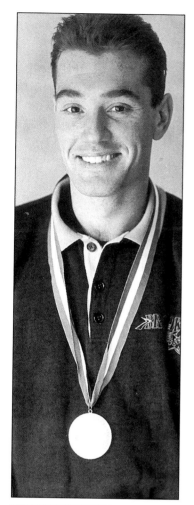

Passing Verrill's Fish and Chip shop, on High Street, Headland, during a 1950s walking race.

Tony Morrell, (left) another top-rated Hartlepool athlete, who won a bronze medal in the 1990 Indoor European Championships 1,500 metres event.

Top billiards player Bob Close in typical action pose.

ROWNTREES OF CHURCH STREET, WEST HARTLEPOOL

FOR THE BEST IN **Duffle Coats** Men's and Teenagers' WELLINGTONS

TELEPHONE 'MAIL' P

CLOUGH WILL MEET 'POOLS TOMORROW

HARTLEPOOLS UNITED are still without a manager . . . at least for one more day. Brian Clough, the former England, Middlesbrough, and Sunderland centre-forward, was to have met 'Pools Chairman, Mr. Ernest Ord, today, when it was expected he would be offered the Victoria Ground position (writes Sentinel).

But the meeting had to be called off when it was learned that Mr. Ord was confined to bed.

"He is not feeling well," Mrs. Ord told me, "but there is a chance that he may be up and about tomorrow."

Clough, who wants to get into football management, was at Roker Park, Sunderland, this morning finalizing arrangements for his testimonial game on Wednesday evening.

"I am now meeting Mr. Ord tomorrow," he said. "He told me he was feeling unwell, and we agreed to postpone today's meeting."

WILL STAY AT SOUTHEND

I understand that former 'Pools chief, Alvan Williams, was approached. But as he has only recently been appointed general manager at Southend, the move understandably did not bear fruit.

Former 'Pools player, Len Richley, another applicant for the Victoria Ground job, is now favourite to land the post of secretary at Bury.

Meanwhile, Geoff Twentyman, the deposed 'Pools "boss," has had his name linked with the trainer-coach's job at Workington. He told me today that he had also had an offer from a firm in Carlisle. But he is keeping an open mind at present, and will not decide for another day or two.

Storton suspended for 14 days

'POOLS UNITED right-back Stan Storton has been

BRIAN CLOUGH, as the fans will see him for the last time on Wednesday when he plays in his testimonial match at Roker Park.

It was a memorable day for Hartlepools United when North-East soccer legend Brian Clough became their manager in October 1965. His travels later took him to fame and fortune via Derby County and Nottingham Forest but his links with 'Pools remained strong and he is shown enjoying a game from the directors' box.

Famous 'Pools names from the past: late manager Gus McLean pictured signing Des McPartland in 1969; two pictures of former captain, Derby County and Nottingham Forest star John McGovern; (opposite page) 1960s star Terry Bell with trainer John Simpson; 1980s hero Bob Newton who scored the dramatic Cup goals against Crystal Palace; and former England, Liverpool and Arsenal star Ray Kennedy who played a major part in keeping Hartlepool United in the Football League.

A novel way of training for these 1970s Hartlepool United stars Allan Goad, Ron Young, Denis White, Neil Warnock and Alan Parry.

How long to go? Worried team officials consult their watches during another gripping game at the Victoria Ground.

Who says it's a glamorous life being a football reporter! This super 1969 snap of the Hartlepool United press box includes well-known journalists Arthur Pickering, then the *Mail's* 'Sentinel' now of Channel 3 North-East, and Jack Fletcher, together with former Middlesbrough star, George Hardwick.

Those were the days! Mounted police help control the crowds before a 1950s Hartlepools United-Darlington FA Cup game.

One of the happiest days in the history of Hartlepool United as the team clinches promotion in 1990-91. They were actually promoted from the old Division Four up to Division Three but, following the formation of the Premier League, started the next season in Division Two!

Some problems never change! Club officials Mal Kirby and Stan Hillhouse tackle a frozen pitch.

One of Hartlepool United's most loyal servants, Brian Honour, meets one of his own idols, England and Newcastle United star Peter Beardsley, during his successful testimonial game.

Happier times for troubled England star Paul Gascoigne as he visits the Victoria Ground shortly after his triumphant World Cup '90.

Motorbike racing at the Victoria Ground in the mid-1930s, a 1960s aerial shot and Victoria Park in all its modern-day splendour.

Ian Botham
and Graham
Gooch are just
two of the
sporting
legends who
have played
first-class
cricket at
Hartlepool's
Park Drive
during the
1990s.

Legendary Hartlepool boxing champ Teddy Gardner shapes up to Battling Manners.

Days to Remember

What better way to celebrate a Royal Coronation or other special occasion than by roasting an ox as these photographs, (the two above and following three overleaf) taken at various stages of the century, starting in 1911, prove.

Alma Street gets busy with the bunting on Coronation Day, 1953.

Hartlepool has enjoyed its fair share of royal visits over the years and here are just a few special moments: A trendy Princess Anne meets Hartlepool College of Art students after officially opening the town's new Middleton Grange Shopping Centre in May 1970 as police cars help control the swelling crowds.

1977 was another royal year in Hartlepool's history when thousands lined the streets to welcome the Queen during her Silver Jubilee year as she officially opened the town's Civic Centre and named *The Scout* lifeboat.

Hartlepool welcomes the Queen during her Silver Jubilee year tour.

Prince Philip chats to dignitaries during his tour of HMS *Warrior* in 1980.

When it comes to the royals, there's no one more popular than Princess Diana, who visited Hartlepool in 1986 with the Prince of Wales, as the photograph of her cheering fans shows.

Her Majesty the Queen last visited the town in May 1993 when she landed from the royal yacht *Britannia* to officially open the multi-million pound Marina development.

Her Majesty the Queen's visit to the Marina development.

Madness, Lindisfarne and Dr and the Medics were just three of the top pop acts who delighted fans with their performances at Dock Rock in 1986. Unfortunately the ambitious event lost thousands of pounds due to poor attendances.

This aerial shot shows the sparse attendance at Dock Rock in 1986.

Locals at The Queen public house will never forget the day Maureen the thirsty elephant popped in for a quick pint in 1989.

Carnivals have always been popular in Hartlepool and this terrific 1954 photograph shows the Town Moor event in full swing.

It was certainly a day to remember for brave Hartlepool heart and lung transplant recipient Mandy Andrews when she met her idols, comedians Cannon and Ball.

Little did young Hartlepool actor Philip Middlemiss dream he would become one of television's favourite pin-up boys when he won the part of ladies' man, bookie Des Barnes in top soap *Coronation Street*.

Hartlepool rock guitarist Janick Gers quickly found fame and fortune when he joined heavy metal supergroup Iron Maiden.

Top '60s singing star
Sandie Shaw lives up
to her name during a
fleeting visit to
Seaton Carew.

Glamorous beauty
Sabrina bowls the fans
over during an early 1960s
visit.

Nightclub boss Ron Trotter meets gorgeous *Top of the Pops'* dancers Pan's People.

Hartlepool's top cartoonist Reg Smythe whose famous character Andy Capp is read daily in the *Daily Mirror* and the Hartlepool *Mail*.

One of the more bizarre incidents of recent years was the brazen theft of the bronze Boer War statue from the town's Ward Jackson Park – leaving just his boots.

Your Mail

It's been an amazing few years for your favourite evening read which has found it leading the way in newspaper technology.

The following photographs show how the old 'hot metal' production process – not to mention reporters' typewriters – have now been replaced by a new multi-million pound computerised, full colour press and editorial system.

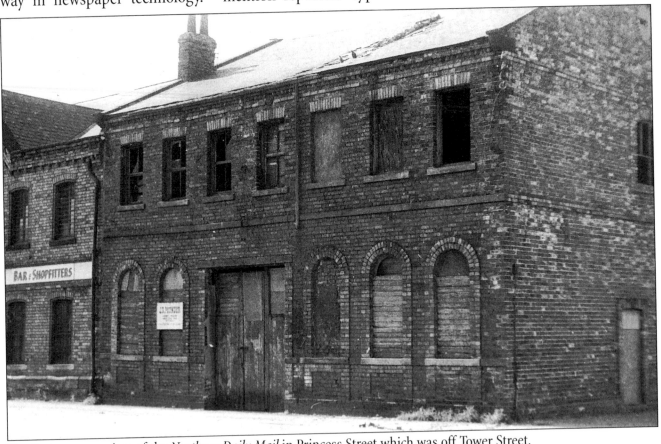

The first ever premises of the *Northern Daily Mail* in Princess Street which was off Tower Street.

Three Views of the *Mail* premises in West House, Clarence Road.

Compositors, press room staff, foundry and distribution workers striving to get the paper out on time when we produced the *Mail* by hot metal method.

Reporters first with the news in the 1970s.

Your high-powered, high-tech daily newspaper of today with its impressive new offices and multi-million pound press.

Another view of the presses at the *Mail* and the high-tech PCs now used for the digital production of the pages.